Baitfish Jubilee

Charles Luden
&
Steve Boint

Scurfpea
Publishing L.L.C.

Copyright © Scurfpea Publishing, 2021. All rights, including electronic, are reserved by the authors and publisher.

First edition 2021.

Cover photograph by Charles Luden.
Title page photograph by Steve Boint.

Scurfpea Publishing LLC
P.O. Box 46
Sioux Falls, SD 57101
scurfpeapublishing.com
editor@scurfpeapublishing.com

Poems

Backyard
by Charles Luden

When I Think of You I Think Forever 1
Saturday Night 2
Sunday Morning Note To Certain Friends 3
Untitled Poem – Number Lost 4
Marvels of Yes 5
"Nothing in my pocket but dark wind" 6
"I went downtown and came back" 7
"There will be flavors at night" 8
Notebook Entry Page 12 9
"Right now light rain" 10
His Wife is Shorter than his Daughter 11
Poem for You: Number 1 12
Poem for You: Number 2 13
Poem of Substantiation 14
Replacements 15
"It is still Wednesday" 16
Contours of Jeopardy 17
"I just had a small glass of red wine . . ." 18
Kicking Through Happy Dust on the Way 19
Decoding a Small Utopia 20
Blurred 21

"The mind shuffles back and forth" 22
Phone Greeting 23
"A light snow is not falling" 24
Cool Scalp 25
"Oh, why Christmas?" 26
Shaken 27
Gas It Up 28
Poem of Justice 29
Thursday Afternoon 30
You 31
"Sloppy dogs splashing by" 32
Friends Meeting 33
Untitled Action 34
The Shy Woodpecker 35
A Poem of Solitude Written in Public 36
The Outdoorsman versus The Indoorsman 37
Explicate This 38
"What am I hiding from by drinking wine?" 39
As I Am 40
Saturday 41
"A girl wrote a book" 42
A Short Story 43
"She's a doily maker" 44
A Day of Work A Night of Thought 45
"They waited in a bus" 46
Immediate Poem 47
"You saw through me" 48
"A farting dog, or the sound of my stomach" 49
Like This Like That 50
A Future in a Layer of Dirt 51
Monday 52
Reader's Block or Anticipation? 53
"The wounded poem appears" 54
Glory 55
To My Poet Friend 56

About Charles Luden 57

Jubilee
by Steve Boint

Night Garden 59
"She sits outside" 60
Monday Morning 61
"Bananas, apples" 62
"Corralled vegetables" 63
"Especially on nights like this" 64
"Sometimes private jets" 65
"Wings of birds landing" 66
Tuesday In the Park 67
"South wind roars through maple leaves" 68
Row House on Aspen Street, Second Floor 69
"This is the time" 70
"Crows laugh at us" 71
"Her cat rests in spikenard" 72
East of Summit Avenue Above 25th St. 73
"That wildfire-red moon floats" 74
Purple Explosions 75
"Nights like these, my toes curl" 76
"Cottonwood puffs thread" 77
Peanut Butter and Geodes 78
10 p.m. 79
"Saunter with me as" 80
Discovery 564 81
"The night was orange halogen" 82
night of the blizzard 83
"Hollyhock husks shiver" 84
8 a.m. December 25 85
"Knees creak beneath winter" 86
One Man With No Audience 87
"Crisium or Serenitatis grabs my eye" 88
Somewhere Else 89
"Assassin bugs crouch" 90
"Sporadic fireflies" 91

"Cicadas and lawnmowers deafen" 92
While Weeding 93
Clouds Race East 94
fall 95
"Blue sky – very blue" 96
Quiet 97
"Thunderheads remain remote" 98
Entranced 99
"There is a ballet" 100
Virtuoso 101
"Sparrows splash the old" 102
"Found the old rose weak" 103
"Beneath cicadas" 104
Blooming Bindweed 105
Happy Labor Day 106
Friends 107
"Windbrush and petals" 108
"Those two distant birds" 109
"A moonless midnight:" 110
"Three feet below hollyhock blooms" 111
"Grey skies wave behind rows of brown poplar" 112
"Down rubber-clad rivers of electrons" 113

About Steve Boint 114

Get ready
now turn the page
in silence

– C. L.

Backyard

When I Think of You I Think Forever

The journey has been long
Yet it's not done
In the wind we feel
In the mind we know
A smile bounces back

    Charles Luden
    Feb 2, 2019
    at Dunn Brothers Coffee

Saturday Night

The cold rain comes
You come
We go
My money goes
You go
I come home

    Charles Luden
    Nov 6, 1977
    at home

Sunday Morning Note To Certain Friends

I realize you are in church now
while I'm walking around looking at the sky
as birds fly over unknowing their freedom
to see secrets below....

    Charles Luden
    March 10, 2019
    at Dunn Brothers Coffee

Untitled Poem – Number Lost

Sitting reading diagrams
on December window frost
I shiver then bark
back at the neighbor's
small dog

> Charles Luden
> June 27, 2019
> at Granite City Food & Brewery

Marvels of Yes

"No" does not compare
to your eyes and
soft sweater
"Yes" is all that
should be said
when the door opens

>> Charles Luden
>> April 26, 2018
>> at Granite City Food & Brewery

Nothing in my pocket but dark wind
and and and you are still
in the next room

>	Charles Luden
>	January 2, 2020
>	at Granite City Food & Brewery

I went downtown and came back
I went to Lewis Drug Eastgate and came back
I went to Lewis Drug Westgate and came back
I went to Sunshine and came back
I went to Taco Johns E 10th and came back
I went to Renner and came back
I went to the Alpine Inn and came back
I went to Joe Foss Field and came back
So far I can come back from wherever I go

    Charles Luden
    July 18, 2021
    at home

There will be flavors at night
and in the morning
perhaps not the same
Let them describe a future
yearned for
each time you turn over
in the bed of serenity

        Charles Luden
        Feb 14, 2020
        at Granite City Food & Brewery

Notebook Entry Page 12

Was disappointed today.
Saw a street sweeper working
my neighborhood while leaving
Burger King.
Upon getting home noticed
no vehicles parked on my block.
Tossing a couple pulled weeds
into the gutter I sat
and waited.
Alas, it did not come.

      Charles Luden
      August 8, 2020
      at home

Right now light rain
Earlier a slice of pie on the patio –
cherry tart on the tongue
Mosquitoes not hatched yet
A calm day
Then the one I love calls

    Charles Luden
    May 3, 2018
    at Granite City Food & Brewery

His Wife is Shorter than his Daughter

Sitting across
from the family dog
begging for biscuits
they smile and recite
algebraic formulas
of nature's mysteries
as rain wets their hair

> Charles Luden
> June 30, 2016
> at Granite City Food & Brewery

Poem for You: Number 1

Coffee, rum, chocolate, and cherries
guide the answer for the quiver
in your soul.
Black air expelled in glee!

>Charles Luden
>January 18, 2018
>at Granite City Food & Brewery

Poem for You: Number 2

There is no hurry...
    Nowhere to go
I've not been to before
except into your arms
    that dangle
There is no hurry...

        Charles Luden
        January 18, 2018
        at Granite City Food & Brewery

Poem of Substantiation

On the ground
small stones galore
pressing our backs
A dog across the street barks
I imagine
Let's look

        Charles Luden
        July 27, 2017
        at Granite City Food & Brewery

Replacements

Today looks to be a good day
to buy a new wooden toilet seat.
A new pair of gloves as well.
North wind is brisk.

>	Charles Luden
>	November 14, 2007
>	at home

It is still Wednesday
in this part of town
Over there – who knows?

        Charles Luden
        September 5, 2018
        at Granite City Food & Brewery

Contours of Jeopardy

Orange followed by blue
followed by grey
Or Julie followed by Bill
followed by Lisa
Or the SUV full of
lunch sacks and a beer cooler
with no beach near

> Charles Luden
> June 29, 2003 & July 4, 2003
> at home

I just had a small glass of red wine and a Twinkie.
Yum.

    Charles Luden
    April 14, 2020
    at home

Kicking Through Happy Dust on the Way to
Cyclops General Hospital

It's a nice morning
and seems to be getting nicer
with each step
Brown birds in every direction
small bees too
Heading to work
Do I still have to work?
My accountant says I do
I think she imagines
possibilities

       Charles Luden
       October 26, 2019
       at Dunn Brothers Coffee

Decoding a Small Utopia

My red car is not white
Repeat
My silver car is not white
Repeat
My green car is not white
Let me compose myself
and tell how it is
The above is all true

>Charles Luden
November 17, 2016
at Granite City Food & Brewery

Blurred

The ukulele is out of tune
as we sing along
to a song unrhymed
but peaceful
unlike the twisted present
requiring self-reliant escapism

    Charles Luden
    April 20, 2017
    at home

The mind shuffles back and forth
between then and here
It is again alive
like you thought
Nothing could go wrong
'cause nothing is
gone too
leaving what is not known

        Charles Luden
        January 24, 2020
        at Granite City Food & Brewery

Phone Greeting

You didn't really do that, did you?
Come on, tell me you didn't.

> Charles Luden
> November 2, 2006
> at Black Sheep Coffee

A light snow is not falling
The sun lowers behind a big tree
Your smile is large
Please repeat it often
Beside me it glows again
a gift to the hearted and heartless
See deep now again

    Charles Luden
    December 10, 2006
    In my Dodge Neon
    parked somewhere in Sioux Falls.

Cool Scalp

Feels like I took my hat off
Oh, I did
It's in my coat pocket
December is out the window

> Charles Luden
> December 12, 2019
> at Granite City Food & Brewery

Oh, why Christmas?
Why not?
A light in the year
yet somber for multitudes
Let's clap!

    Charles Luden
    June 19. 1997
    at Spezia

Shaken

Let me sing now to you
sinking in that chair
No lake out the window
only golden grass
and a torn sombrero

>   Charles Luden
>   February 16, 2021
>   at home

Gas It Up

I've bought enough gas in my lifetime
It's expensive now
Shouldn't need anymore
Could walk or stay home
Let others drive
Oh, but the feel behind the wheel!

    Charles Luden
    May 2, 2007
    at Sankofa Coffee

Poem of Justice

I know hope
Along the green field

Water swishes
Clear to there

A yes in a mind
No other feels

      Charles Luden
      May 13, 2020
      at home

Thursday Afternoon

I hear a horse in the street
Oh, I'm mistaken
It's just the dripping coffee maker

    Charles Luden
    May 24, 2007
    at Michelle's Coffee

You

Each month begins with 1
and ends at the right time
This happens even in your absence
Now the breeze is kind
as you come near
wafting perfume into the yard

      Charles Luden
      Jan 5, 2007
      at Black Sheep Coffee and Spezia

Sloppy dogs splashing by
You need a phone call
could be said
Relieve me too
I know who from black cherries
are served
Now let's talk
then finger the dog collar
beside the curb
One did not get away
Yes it did

    Charles Luden
    October 10, 2019
    at home

Friends Meeting

We are public people
No one ever comes to our houses
No one is invited
We sit at coffee houses
bars and restaurants
We talk, look out windows
watch things
If it weren't for public places
we wouldn't know one another
So where do you live?

>Charles Luden
>May 23, 2007
>at Black Sheep Coffee

Untitled Action

Run fast
get there
sometime

The future
is not
now

Of course
shoes make
the difference

> Charles Luden
> March 8, 2007
> at Champps

The Shy Woodpecker

No
It's just the way
he is

>   Charles Luden
>   May 19, 2007
>   at Black Sheep Coffee

A Poem of Solitude Written in Public

It's getting dark
too dark to see
yet a bird flutters
in a bush

        Charles Luden
        March 11, 2016
        at Granite City Food & Brewery

The Outdoorsman versus The Indoorsman

One does
The other watches

>Charles Luden
November 21, 2019
at Granite City Food & Brewery

Explicate This

There was a time
Now there still is

Your body is still yours

The mouse on the floor
is small
Your face wet and clean

The axe in the corner
never used

>Charles Luden
>January 27, 2021
>at home

What am I hiding from by drinking wine?
What am I diving into by drinking coffee?

    Charles Luden
    October 28, 2006
    at Black Sheep Coffee

As I Am

You can't call my name
because you don't know it
You are elfin almost free
walking beside the bright day
It's so light you can't be seen
How do I know you're there?
Maybe I don't
Let's pretend

>Charles Luden
December 26, 2019
at Granite City Food & Brewery

Saturday

A pocketful of dimes
A fistful of quarters
A handful of water
A pailful of birdseed
A bucketful of twigs
A bunch of purple plums
A tankful of gas
A bagful of peanuts
A controversy of poets

> Charles Luden
> July 17, 2021
> at home

A girl wrote a book
became a woman
and my friend
Still wonders why
we can forget

    Charles Luden
    September 13, 2018
    at Granite City Food & Brewery

A Short Story

You only made a hundred thousand
with your million dollar face
Now you crawl with vengeance
the morning after

    Charles Luden
    April 25, 2008
    at Black Sheep Coffee

She's a doily maker
on a porch swing
mint julep on the table
a soldier on her mind
Tomorrow a letter in her mailbox
saying hello then
goodbye

        Charles Luden
        February 25, 2016
        at Granite City Food & Brewery

A Day of Work
A Night of Thought

Is it almost empty, very empty,
or just empty?
Work does that on hot days,
on cold ones too.
Toil, sweat, shivers.
Is it how you are,
or how I am?
I see you are wearing a mask.
Me too.
Does it make the dust easier to bear?
It still gets in the eyes,
so I'm not seeing well.
My hands shake too.
Fingers inside something that
has no feel.
Perhaps they are next to nothing.
I used to work in hot water;
now I pour mild acid into Nalgene bottles.
I once asked my boss if he preferred
Erlenmeyer or Florence flasks.
He said, I'm a number cruncher; use the
ones you like.

    Charles Luden
    Jan 18, 2021
    at home

They waited in a bus
Would not get out
Why?
Would not answer cell phone
Why?
That is all I know

    Charles Luden
    September 8, 2021
    at home

Immediate Poem

My scalp has a burning sensation
yet looking cool
hair almost gone
in the quick breeze
so I put on a hat

A car ride to the Night Cafe
is a life saver
right now
almost midnight
I face the wall

      Charles Luden
      April 7, 2021
      at home

You saw through me
and I through you
I kept the secret
so not to spoil the idea

        Charles Luden
        January 7, 2007
        at Z'kota Grill (now Hardee's)

A farting dog, or the sound of my stomach
woke me slightly since I wasn't quite asleep,
yet near to a dream. A waking dream perhaps
of rumbling as a vehicle slow on crunchy gravel
with a holey muffler. Then the animal, or my stomach
brought me up from left side down to propped on
my pillow chair at the headboard to listen to noises
real or imagined as wisps of wind in the branches
out the window, or that dog.

    Charles Luden
    February 17, 1997
    at home 2:30 PM

Like This Like That

Like petunias in the sun
the moon is bright
tonight
I see
You have a clean face
except for a little smudge
of mascara
said the snake
moving towards
water

    Charles Luden
    February 18, 2016
    at Granite City Food & Brewery

A Future in a Layer of Dirt

Who will tell the birds the old stories
of how man fed them
after man has gone?

>   Charles Luden
>   March 27, 2016
>   at home

Monday

You cannot take me to bed.
I'm already there.
Join me if you wish.
I'm positioned not to snore.
Squeeze my ankle to awaken
laughs inside.

    Charles Luden
    June 21, 2021
    at home

Reader's Block or Anticipation ?

Sometimes I can't even read
a five line poem completely
before stopping to rest
or dream about where
the final line will go
or perhaps finish it
in my head on my own
or fall asleep

      Charles Luden
      March 2, 2021
      at home 2:00 PM

The wounded poem appears
from almost nowhere
Makes me wish for more sleep
next to your stolen prayer books
Each morning on our knees
our hands speak endless controversy

    Charles Luden
    November 5, 2015
    at home

Glory

Water runs over my feet
on the way to your feet
Are we sitting near the Falls
of the Sioux
or just thinking about
how long it took to get here
without the sunshine?
Touch my hand so I know
I do not dream of your feel
but know it now
hard as I think
you think next
to me

>	Charles Luden
>	Feb 14, 2019
>	at Granite City Food & Brewery

Originally published in *Without Fear of Infamy*,
edited by Brad and Jennifer Soule (2019)

To My Poet Friend
for Steve Boint

There's a seesaw of bananas above your head
balancing on the spine of your current book
It's up on the left then down to level
and past the embossed title
pointing to the basement
where words come from

        Charles Luden
        September 4, 2014
        at Granite City Food & Brewery

Charles Luden has been reading and writing poetry since the late 1960s. He is a 1971 graduate from Augustana University. His working career was spent in chemical laboratories. Also, he played drums in various combos including Exploding Parakeet, Gypsy and the Outlaws, No Direction, Chord on Blue, and Habitual Groove of It. His published books include *Virgin Death*, *West of Venus: punk love poems*, *World of If*, *Blue Thirsty*, and *Drilling the Hooves of Sheep*. He received the 2004 Sioux Falls Mayor's Award for Literary Arts.

Jubilee

Night Garden

Someone dropped the moon into the water dish.
Hope dry rabbits won't mind.
South wind curls through brown-eyed susan.
Nightshade winds around lilac long past bloom.
We could wait together
for the shush of sphinx moth wings;
would you mind?

Steve Boint

Especially on nights like this,
front steps ripple in a cool breeze of hope.
Second-story windows ignite
then blinds are pulled tight.
This world reclines
into another attempt,
tomorrow.
The musk of boiling asphalt gives way
to dust lifted by dancing shoes.
Join me?
We can take turns leading.

    Steve Boint

Monday Morning

Bang and rattle.
Clipped voices.
Neighbors load themselves
into a large metal truck.
Three grackles perform
high-wire surveillance
and remain unmoved
as the moving van departs.

    Steve Boint

Bananas, apples
and cat food on the counter.
Bird seed by the door.

    Steve Boint

Corralled vegetables.
Fenced flowers.
With wide-brimmed hat
and squirt bottle,
he rides herd
through suburban shadows.

    Steve Boint

She sits outside
on humid summer evenings
as the roar of neighborhood parties,
ambiance of distant traffic,
and high-pitched rasp of insects
drown the cicadas of her mind.

    Steve Boint

Sometimes private jets
well-lit, low and smooth
curling out of dark.
Cargo props the same.

Thursdays, late and high,
red dots,
horizon to horizon,
some red-eye flyover.

Nearer soil: fireflies
hunt bushes, darting bats
hunt treetops. We rest
on grass fresh with dew.

    Steve Boint

Wings of birds landing
mimic the rustle and rhythm
of newspapers closed;
she squints soft into morning.

    Steve Boint

Tuesday In the Park

Dogs with people walk by.
A cockatoo riding a cute shoulder
    bobs its head in passing.
Bees whip left to right,
    except for a few going right to left.
Ants everywhere;
    one crawls over my shoe.
This is a good place.

    Steve Boint

South wind roars through maple leaves
and fights a lumbering, whining propeller plane.
Uninterested, above,
a concave moon fills with dark
and falls slowly westward.

    Steve Boint

Row House on Aspen Street
    Second Floor, November

A string of LEDs around a window
and from the street you can look up, evenings,
and catch her wrinkled, rainbowed face
sheltering behind a coffee mug.
I like to think her eyes smile.

    Steve Boint

This is the time
of biting flies.
Dry birdbaths dot brown yards.
Dust balloons
behind running dogs.
Should we chase them
or the ice cream truck?

    Steve Boint

Crows laugh at us
as our delivery trucks beep backwards
and leaf blowers roar to drown lawn mowers.
That old man rests in his frayed lawn chair
wondering what squirrels holler down from trees.

    Steve Boint

Her cat rests in spikenard
against the alley
where rusted tomato cages,
twisted chicken wire,
and a wheelbarrow missing a tire
testify to dreams in energetic youth.
This summer, she picks garbage
from fading flower beds and wonders
at the previously-unnoticed beauty of weeds.

    Steve Boint

East of Summit Avenue Above 25th St.

From behind cedar fencing,
a dog barks staccato wisps
into blue aether.
A barely-rolling mail truck
zigzags its GPS-driven route,
three times passing a gray man
shambling forward while
thinking about squirrels.
Directly in front of each house, he turns
to face its porch and smiles –
they won't know his name, but
they'll all have his photo
briefly, an electronic wisp
in the security aether.

    Steve Boint

That wildfire-red moon floats
slowly
through cold-flame firefly trails.
From backyards,
faint whispers
between friends
of one sort or another
filter through
promises and pleas from insects.

    Steve Boint

Purple Explosions

Way up high,
leaving green,
petals rain
pink and red and white.
Down here,
everything explodes
purple
except
burning dandelion suns.

    Steve Boint

Nights like these, my toes curl
over that Great Divide.
I almost hear your voice.

    Steve Boint

Cottonwood puffs thread
bloom ends of dames rocket
waving above aging daisies
white, yellow, brown.
Cardinals, wrens, robins call from
mulberry-laden branches,
lilacs around the birdbath,
crab-apple-heavy trees.
Squirrels scold that I shouldn't
record this Chagall world:
no one will believe.

  Steve Boint

Peanut Butter and Geodes

It's amazing, the zing
of breakfast sunlight
splashing between rocky windowsills
and your ancient steel toaster.
Unrhymable juice.
Unneeded grape jelly.
A bee taps glass arrhythmically.
I could get used to this.

    Steve Boint

10 p.m.

and the insect cloud swarms
4-stories thick, judging by wheeling bats.
Like them,

he does his part, smashing mosquitoes
against his forehead
like beer cans.

    Steve Boint

Saunter with me as
harsh cicada calls echo
through mulberry rain.
We might notice what we've missed.
We might stumble over peace.

    Steve Boint

Discovery 564

on County Road 27
on my Suzuki GT750

butterflies are edible

    Steve Boint

The night was orange halogen
and the wind, ice –
a sherbet midnight.

    Steve Boint

night of the blizzard

wind strained
through maple, walnut, ash, mulberry, pine
voice of earth
voice of sky
a choir extending for acres
sections roar while others rest
bass, baritone, tenor

hidden amidst the baroque oratorio fifty feet above
nested squirrels bob
in the center of the choir

ground-bound
surrounded from above
my desire consumed, lifted, dashed
cowering yet reaching upward

alive

    Steve Boint

Hollyhock husks shiver
in this wind. A pair of sparrows
launches from dormant grape.
Beneath the rose rising
brown through last night's snow
a rabbit braves dusting gusts.
Christmas is gentle this year.

    Steve Boint

8 a.m. December 25

Through filtering snowflakes, faintly,
church bells (prerecorded, automated,
broadcast through permanently-mounted speakers)
ring a hauntingly impersonal blessing
down neighborhood streets. Sprinkling
last night's leftover bread crumbs and salad
beneath our tarnished copper birdbath,
I glance toward a rabbit ready
to bolt from the yard's far corner,
"For you. Merry Christmas."

    Steve Boint

Knees creak beneath winter
skies dimmer, greenish –
he remembers their truth
clearly as they used to blow past.
No reason to be out in this,
but he smiles at the clean
remembrance of air.

    Steve Boint

One Man With No Audience

Early Sunday afternoon,
dogs dragged masters
past randomly-spaced, ice-hung evergreens.
You were with me;
snow crunched underfoot.
Faintly, from a distant band shell
Amazing Grace
emanated over barren drifts
and abandoned playgrounds,
an empty ice rink
and neighboring homes.
Chickadees sang their own joy.

       Steve Boint

Crisium or Serenitatis grabs my eye,
a 250,000-mile-long slap
from behind aether-black hackberry leaves
dancing, dancing.
Always darkness shifting.
The light, too, shifts
yet remains empty of life.
Something rustles in shadow
of bergamot and brown-eyed susan.
For a moment, brighter than the moon,
a moth's eye catches mine.
I click my flashlight off,
apologize.

  Steve Boint

Somewhere Else

Sol sets early behind brownstone and brick.
Shoppers are replaced by drinkers and grazers
shuffling through fetid August air, clipped
conversations, car alarms, and horns.
Oblivious, benched beneath an amber streetlight,
she casts herself into a paperback.

    Steve Boint

Assassin bugs crouch
one milkweed leaf south
of a spider's trap.
Wasps threaten everything,
one bloom / one leaf
at a time

    Steve Boint

Sporadic fireflies
hover low beneath the weight
of stale, soggy air.
Our amber moon failed to rise,
but faint stars carry magic.

    Steve Boint

Cicadas and lawnmowers deafen,
but clouds drift soft,
humid breezes brush warm skin
and pastel flowers light the sidewalk's edge.
At the park across the street,
squirrels tease dogs.

    Steve Boint

While Weeding

Tap,
soft but insistent,
on my bald spot.
Finger snaps
low around me.
"Here!"
"Look!"
"Here!"
And so I do.
And so I sit
watching bobbing leaves
and swaying stems
in my garden
under the rain.

      Steve Boint

Clouds Race East

Down the block,
that old wooden gate swings loose,
banging and groaning.
North wind hints at autumn
and hackberry and maple whisper
excitedly about the change.
In his neighbor's window box,
petunias toss but hold their own.
Front-step-sitting, coffee in hand,
he smiles.

    Steve Boint

fall

you drove away
red car and flurry
red, yellow, orange leaves
waving

I was slapped
by a yellow elm leaf
falling

laughing
knowing
they will return
and you

        Steve Boint

Blue sky – very blue.
Tan grass. Brown dirt. But blue sky –
blue, blue, blue, O, blue.

    Steve Boint

Quiet

No one is
coming here –
I know that.
Still I wait.
Still, I sit.
What better
would I do?

    Steve Boint

Thunderheads remain remote,
white on light-hearted blue.
On the corner,
a lawn mower and then leaf blower howl.
Mid block, she waters window petunias
and thinks about hail.
An old Toyota idles
in our driveway.

    Steve Boint

Entranced

Lolling and bobbing,
surging and swaying, warm wind
moves the trees . . . and me.

    Steve Boint

There is a ballet
of discarded shopping bags
this blustery day.

    Steve Boint

Virtuoso

Faintly
from some window half opened
or a hidden backyard,
Beethoven's 5th
twisting in wind,
accompanied by birds –
the blues version
on harmonica.

      Steve Boint

Sparrows splash the old
bird bath half sunken
in the soggy backyard
and the sun reflects: a hundred
stars nestled in grass.

Steve Boint

Found the old rose weak
in the shade of ferns. Wonder
if it can be moved
without hurting rose or fern.
Change must be thoroughly planned.

    Steve Boint

Beneath cicadas,
fireflies light languid trails. Bats
cartwheel through still air.

    Steve Boint

Blooming Bindweed

on purple sage,
yellow clover corralling tan-headed brome.
What do you dream?

    Steve Boint

Happy Labor Day

Car doors slam greetings
echoed by voices.
Grills fill almost-clear skies with aroma.
This aging afternoon gives way
to a young evening.
Through the final holiday of summer,
our neighborhood dances.
What's that you say?
I wouldn't disagree.

    Steve Boint

Friends

Around that table they sat,
last night,
five old men reminiscing
about today. Wondering if
yesterday will survive
expectations, drinking
as much as they couldn't.

    Steve Boint

Windbrush and petals
paint September afternoons
in confusion.

    Steve Boint

Those two distant birds
heading south are unable
to fly in a vee.

    Steve Boint

A moonless midnight:
crickets play to blackness, drunk
voices on the wind.

    Steve Boint

Three feet below hollyhock blooms,
engulfed in bumble-bee minuets,
engrossed by passing salsify puffs,
cross-legged and humming,
she waits for nothing,
summoned by no one.
Finally, mornings are good.

    Steve Boint

Grey skies wave behind rows of brown poplar.
Black dots wing from sky to trees.
Hints of red in evening's grey,
as of glory almost achieved,
then dark.

    Steve Boint

Down rubber-clad rivers of electrons,
squirrels transport hopes, dreams, prayers,
maybe walnuts –
things too real for digital streams.
On streets, the unheeding
roar loud engines into oblivion.
But along alleys,
butterflies and birds gather
to the monkish chant
as those packets are gnawed open,
rhythmically,
one at a time.

    Steve Boint

After high school, Steve Boint hitchhiked across the northern U.S. He then settled into gaining multiple academic degrees and spending multiple decades teaching chemistry, astronomy, and physics at the high school and undergraduate levels. Along the way, and with much help, he built a radio telescope that spots cold clouds of hydrogen in space, produced and sold art at local galleries, and founded Scurfpea Publishing. His published works include: *Frail As Paper*, *Physicist at the Window*, *Elsewhere*, *Did Jesus Die for Dogs?*, *Holiday Street*, *Sketchbook 91.1.1*, *Always Passing Through*, and *Stranded wherever I am*.

Made in the USA
Columbia, SC
02 December 2021